Kenilworth Castle

Richard K Morris

Introduction

Kenilworth Castle is one of the great historical sites of the United Kingdom. It was a royal castle for most of its history, and many of the buildings remain unaltered since the reign of Queen Elizabeth I. Its walls enclose a series of outstanding works of medieval and early Renaissance architecture.

Set on a low sandstone hill at the crossroads of two ancient trackways, the first castle was established in the 1120s by the royal chamberlain, Geoffrey de Clinton. He built most of the Norman great tower and also founded Kenilworth Priory close by. In the early 13th century King John added an outer circuit of stone walls and a dam to hold back a great lake, thus creating one of the most formidable fortresses in the kingdom. It withstood a full-scale siege in 1266.

Subsequently the castle was developed as a palace. John of Gaunt, son of King Edward III, constructed the great hall, with associated apartments and services. In the 15th century the castle was a favoured residence of the Lancastrian kings, who were drawn here by the excellent hunting; King Henry V built a retreat called 'the Pleasance in the Marsh' at the far end of the lake. In 1563 Elizabeth I granted the castle to her favourite, Robert Dudley, earl of Leicester. He converted Kenilworth into a great house for her entertainment, which culminated in 19 days of festivities in 1575.

The castle's fortifications were dismantled in 1650 after the Civil War, and Leicester's Gatehouse was converted into a residence by the Parliamentarian officer, Colonel Hawkesworth. Later the ivy-clad ruins became famous as the setting for Sir Walter Scott's 1821 novel *Kenilworth*, which romanticized the story of Robert Dudley and Elizabeth I. The castle was given by Lord Kenilworth to the town of Kenilworth in 1958, and since 1984 it has been managed by English Heritage.

Above: Robert Dudley, earl of Leicester, from a miniature by Nicholas Hilliard, 1571–4

Facing page: The castle seen from the south, across the meadows that once formed part of the great lake or mere. John of Gaunt's buildings are to the left, Leicester's Building is in the centre and the great tower is to the right

Tour

The spectacular ruins of Kenilworth Castle reveal much of its medieval and Tudor past as a royal residence. The tour begins with the outer defences of the castle, before exploring the magnificent buildings of the inner court, at the heart of the castle: the 12th-century great tower; the great hall and state apartments built by John of Gaunt; and Leicester's Building, the 16th-century apartment block erected for Elizabeth I by Robert Dudley, earl of Leicester. It then takes in the outer court, including Leicester's Gatehouse, which contains an exhibition on Leicester and Elizabeth, the stable block (now housing a café and introductory exhibition), and the outer walls.

For a tour of the recently recreated Elizabethan garden, see page 30.

FOLLOWING THE TOUR

The tour of the castle starts just outside the ticket office and shop. The numbers beside the headings highlight the key points on the tour and correspond with the small numbered plans in the margins.

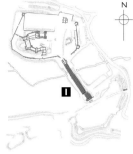

Left: The castle buildings seen from the tiltyard
Below: A scene from the great tournament held at Westminster by Henry VIII on New Year's Day 1511. For jousting, the tiltyard at Kenilworth would have had a barrier like this down the centre, and spectators would have looked on from the towers at each end

Facing page: The southern towers of the inner court, seen from the outer court: the Saintlowe Tower (left), Gaunt's Tower (centre) and the south-west turret of Leicester's Building (right)

▮ EXTERIOR AND OUTLYING FEATURES

The view from just outside the visitor centre provides a splendid visual introduction to the castle. The main buildings stand on a low sandstone hill above the confluence of the Finham and Inchford brooks. When the Norman castle was built in the 1120s, the construction of a causeway across this valley created a dam which held back a lake (known as the mere) to the west. This was vastly enlarged when King John heightened the dam in the early 13th century. A little further down the valley was the abbey pool adjoining Kenilworth Priory, the monastery founded in about 1124 at the same time as the castle (see page 38). The top of the dam was later widened to make it suitable for jousting at tournaments, and by the mid-16th century it was referred to as the 'tiltyard'.

Standing on the tiltyard today, the visitor needs to imagine the mere stretching into the middle distance to the left. Behind lie the remains of the defences and water controls essential to the security and maintenance of the mere. Near the ticket office are the fragmentary remains of the Gallery Tower and its courtyard, part of the gatehouse which guarded the southern end of the dam. It takes its name from a remodelling in the 16th century as a viewing gallery for tournaments. Beyond is the large defensive earthwork of the Brays (in which the car park lies), with the line of its banks and huge ditches now marked by the arc of tall trees. The name is likely to derive from the French 'braie', a military outwork defended by palisades. It was probably built in the first half of the 13th century, but its origins and history warrant further research.

Right: The remains of the twin towers of Mortimer's Tower, the main gatehouse to the medieval castle

Below: Kenilworth Castle as it appeared in 1620, in a 19th-century copy of a lost 17th-century wall-painting at Newnham Paddox House, Warwickshire. It shows the castle with its mere and pools before the dismantling of 1650, the tiltyard (left), the inner court with the lost east range (centre), and the site of the garden (right)

2 MORTIMER'S TOWER

Mortimer's Tower was the main medieval entrance to the castle. It was first given this name by Sir William Dugdale, the 17th-century antiquary, and probably relates to Roger Mortimer, who hosted a tournament at the castle in 1279. It is still possible to make out the two D-shaped towers of the gatehouse, built as part of King John's ring of stone defences for the outer bailey between about 1210 and 1215. Originally the towers were at least one storey higher. They would have had battlements, and were linked by an entrance passage.

In the passage, grooves survive for a portcullis, which would have been operated by a winch in

the room above. A door on each side led to two porter's lodges fitted with fireplaces, according to a survey of the castle made in 1563. King John's gatehouse was built in front of a simpler, 12th-century gatehouse. The walls of this earlier building are preserved at the inner end of the passage, together with another portcullis slot. Even in their mutilated form, both gatehouses are significant survivals of fortifications from their respective periods.

Like much of the castle, Mortimer's Tower was dismantled in 1650, following the Civil War.

3 BASE COURT

Beyond Mortimer's Tower lies the 'base court', the lowest part of the outer court. On the right is the 16th-century stable (see page 28), and beyond the trees in the distance is Leicester's Gatehouse (page 26). The avenue of trees was planted only about 150 years ago, to enhance the picturesque setting of the ruins.

4 INNER COURT

On the higher ground rises the monumental group of buildings of the inner court. The buildings now enclose the court on three sides. To the right is the great tower (or keep) built by Geoffrey de Clinton

in the 1120s, which was at the heart of the defences of the Norman castle, and also served as its main residence. In the centre beyond is the 14th-century great hall, built by John of Gaunt between about 1373 and 1380. The towering block to the left is Leicester's Building, erected to provide private apartments for Elizabeth I in 1571. It was consciously designed as a counterpart to the ancient keep. Together they present a façade to the outer court which is harmonious in overall form yet varied in detail; the massive solidity of the great tower contrasts with the delicate windows of Leicester's Building – a typically Elizabethan conceit.

In the 16th century these two towers were linked by a lower east range, named by Sir William Dugdale 'King Henry's Lodgings', which would have hidden the inner court from view. Built in Henry VIII's reign between about 1530 and 1532, this was a two-storey, timber-framed structure erected on the line of the earlier inner bailey wall, and probably replaced a previous range which had decayed. Its likely purpose was to improve the private apartments and to provide additional lodgings. Window glass brought from London in 1531–2, painted with the badges and arms of the king, was probably intended for this building. It was

South-east turret of the great tower

A Remains of the entrance gate to the inner court

B Portcullis groove

C Scar for the battlemented parapet of the wall-walk

D 16th-century door giving access to the top of the east range

Left: An artist's impression of the east façade of the inner court in about 1575, with Leicester's Building (left), the east range (centre) and the great tower (right). The east range was demolished in 1650, so its details are open to conjecture, and it was probably lower than in this reconstruction (compare with the painting opposite)

N

Right: The south elevation of the great tower, with the forebuilding to the left. The entrance to the forebuilding is a Victorian reconstruction (compare with the old photograph opposite)

Below: One of the fish-tailed arrowloops, part of King John's additions to the top of the great tower

almost certainly remodelled in stone by Leicester about 1571–2, to incorporate his lodgings during the royal visit of 1575. It was demolished when the castle was slighted (made indefensible) in 1650, after the Civil War.

In Tudor times, visitors would have entered the inner court through a gatehouse between the great tower and the east range. In front of the entrance are the foundations of one side of a causeway and the springing for a bridge across the former dry ditch. For the arrival of Elizabeth I on 9 July 1575, this bridge was decorated with gifts symbolizing Roman gods and goddesses, such as weapons (from Mars), wine (Bacchus) and musical instruments (Phoebus), arranged on pairs of posts.

Although the architecture of the inner court ranges in date from the 1120s to the 1570s, a sense of harmony pervades the ensemble. This is due in part to the use of the same mellow red sandstone, from quarries adjacent to the castle. Conscious architectural devices have also been employed, such as the way the tall sloping plinth of the 14th-century hall makes reference to the stepped plinth of the great tower.

5 GREAT TOWER AND FOREBUILDING

Facing the great tower from the centre of the inner court, it is not difficult to appreciate why this massive building was always at the heart of the castle's defence. It was also successively used for residence, administration and entertainment.

Exterior

On the side facing the inner court (the south), three main periods of building are evident. The two main floors were probably built by Geoffrey de Clinton in the 1120s. In the centre section his work extends up to the foot of the arrowloops. Most of the top stage was added by King John about 1210–15 and is characterized by the fish-tailed arrowloops. John was also responsible for a chamber with fine views at the top of the south-west turret. The three Elizabethan grid windows on the first floor were introduced by Robert Dudley, earl of Leicester, about 1570–71, to light a great room for entertaining. At the top of the south-east (right) turret are peg-holes for the square face of the castle clock, which was stopped at two o'clock throughout Elizabeth's visit in 1575.

Forebuilding

Adjoining the great tower on the left is the forebuilding, which provided additional security and a grand ceremonial entry. High above the entry to the forebuilding, abutting the great tower, is the jamb of a tall oriel window, which once lit a fine first-floor chamber. The jamb is decorated with Leicester's badges, the cinquefoil and the ragged staff, and below it is the date '[1]570'. Unusually, these carvings have been done after construction, so the window probably pre-dates 1570 and is an early work for Leicester of about 1569.

The forebuilding is entered through the restored, round-arched doorway. The interior is characterized by the classical arcades of the loggia, inserted in about 1569. They framed a small open courtyard and created a fashionable vestibule to access the great tower and to approach the garden site beyond.

Originally the forebuilding would have been an enclosed space, with a staircase going up to the first-floor entrance into the great tower. If the round-headed door now connecting to the lower floor of the great tower is part of the original 12th-century arrangement, then practical access to the great tower would have been as important a function of the forebuilding as providing defence. Later changes, however, make it impossible now to reconstruct the Norman arrangement in detail. Rooflines on the north face of the corner turret, and large beam-holes in the wall of the great tower, testify to various remodellings of the forebuilding. In the 13th century it was extended north to provide an exterior access to the outer bailey, and later it served as the door to the garden.

From here visitors can either continue with the tour of the great tower or proceed directly to the Elizabethan garden (see page 30).

Great Tower Interior

This monumental building consisted of two lofty floors with a fighting deck above. Its walls are 14 feet (4.3m) thick, as shown by the scars of the north wall, which was demolished in 1649–50. During the 12th century, the great tower was probably the main residence of the castle, centred on a great hall occupying the upper floor. The lower floor of the great tower (where the visitor stands) was separated from the hall above by a wooden ceiling on intermediate supports. The hall

Above: The date '[1]570' carved on the forebuilding. Between the '5' (only partly surviving) and the '7' is a ragged staff held by the arm of a bear; one of his ears is visible above

Left: The loggia leading to the garden, seen from the forebuilding entrance. The arcades framed a small courtyard

Below: This photograph of about 1860 shows the decayed state of the forebuilding and great tower before later 19th-century restoration

Great tower interior, looking east

A Door to the stairs

B Original Norman window

C Ground-floor access to the well

D Spiral staircase

E First-floor doors to the well and south-east turret

F Elizabethan windows inserted into 12th-century apertures

GREAT TOWER AND FOREBUILDING

First floor

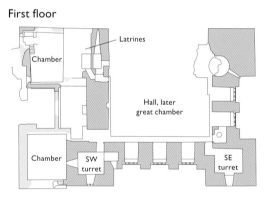

Chamber

Latrines

Hall, later great chamber

Chamber

SW turret

SE turret

Ground floor

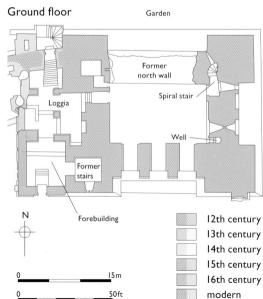

Garden

Former north wall

Spiral stair

Loggia

Well

Former stairs

N

Forebuilding

	12th century
	13th century
	14th century
	15th century
	16th century
	modern

0 — 15m

0 — 50ft

was an undivided space entered from the forebuilding by the large door in the west wall on the first floor, with a massive roof spanning about 30 feet (9m). It was well appointed, with a well in its south-east corner and spiral stairs in the north-east turret giving access to all levels. Latrines in the north-west turret were accessed through the round-arched door in the west wall, close to which is a small, restored 12th-century fireplace.

The hall was lit by large, segmental-arched windows, probably like the restored examples in the west wall. They are likely to be modifications made in the 1170s or 1180s by Henry II and, if reliably restored, are remarkable in size for a 12th-century great tower. Leading off the hall were chambers in the south-east and south-west turrets; the latter turret might have housed a chapel. A payment was made in 1444–5 for adapting the chapel to store 'evidences' (documents), indicating an administrative function for the great tower in the 15th century. Between 1570 and 1571 Leicester remodelled the hall as a great chamber, to serve as the equivalent of an Elizabethan long gallery, where some of his notable collection of paintings might have been displayed (see page 47).

The lower floor originally supplied additional accommodation for the household. The Norman slit window in the east wall shows how dark it would have been before Leicester enlarged the window apertures in the south wall to create an open loggia.

JOHN OF GAUNT'S WORKS

Next to the forebuilding and the great tower are the buildings erected between about 1373 and 1380 for John of Gaunt, the fourth son of Edward III and titular king of Spain. His great hall is the centrepiece, with the Strong Tower and kitchens to the right, and the Saintlowe Tower and the site of the state apartments to the left. Together they represent the finest survival of an English royal palace of the later Middle Ages, and one of the clearest expressions of the organization of a great aristocratic household in the period.

The household was run by the chamberlain, the steward, the treasurer and the clerk of the wardrobe. Gaunt's household numbered over 100 male servants, many of aristocratic birth, whose primary purpose was to maintain the magnificence of his public image.

EVENTS

ENGLISH HERITAGE
Days out worth talking about.

A GRAND MEDIEVAL JOUST
Kenilworth Castle
Saturday 9ᵗʰ & Sunday 10ᵗʰ July 2011

oday you will see a true battle of heroes as four Knights gather at Kenilworth
Castle to take part in a thrilling tournament. Visitors are invited to choose their
hampion - each Knight will be represented by their livery of either blue, red, yellow
r green, representing the North, South, East and West.

Cheer on your favourite in the mounted skill at arms, where the Knights
emonstrate their skill on horseback. Don't forget to visit the English Heritage shop
o purchase your matching t-shirt or flag and enjoy the thrills and spills of the
ighlight of the day, the Joust itself.

ou will also be treated to incredible flying displays performed by Raphael Historic
alconry, plus medieval music from Blast from the Past and mischief from our jester,
Peterkin the Fool. Visit the falconry mews and living history encampments
hroughout the day to meet our medieval re-enactors and learn about what life
would have been like in days gone by.

Please Note!
- When visiting living history displays, please do not touch anything unless invited to by the performers
- For their own safety children must be kept under close supervision
- Please do not cross any tape barriers unless invited to do so by the performers
- Please take your litter home

Visit **www.english-heritage.org.uk/events** or call **0870 3331183**

Left: The great tower and the site of the kitchens, seen from the Strong Tower
Below: Reconstruction of the copper, which was built into the east fireplace of the kitchen (visible in the photograph, left)
Bottom: The late medieval kitchen at Windsor Castle, as depicted by James Stephanoff in the 19th century, gives a good impression of a top-lit kitchen with massive fireplaces like Kenilworth's

s
l was
al guests.
ll wall
f it today
ented
ry, larder,
ll of
e pastry,
erve as

chunks of meat. The copper is a modification, probably introduced in the later 15th century. This kitchen had the capacity to cater for several hundred people if necessary, but the east fireplace alone would have been adequate for the skeleton staff when the lord was not in residence.

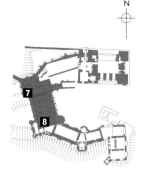

Strong Tower

A Site of the dresser and stairs to the hall

B Entrance to the cellars

C Site of the buttery, pantry and passage from the kitchen to the great hall

D Steward's lodgings and 'Amy Robsart's chamber'

Right: The cellars of the Strong Tower

STRONG TOWER

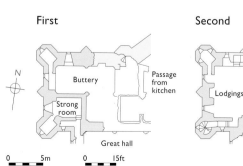

Ground floor

First

Second

containers for food, was probably to the left of the door into the Strong Tower cellars. Beside the exit from the kitchens was a dresser, where the food was arranged before being carried up the stairs (on the line of the present wooden staircase) and through a passage into the hall.

7 STRONG TOWER

The name 'a strong tower' appears in a survey of the castle made in 1545, presumably alluding to the remarkable feature that all its floors were vaulted in stone. The tower's stone-vaulted cellars, which feel like dungeons, actually housed the larders.

A wooden staircase now leads to the first floor of the Strong Tower. Only the western rooms of the tower survive at this level. This floor was occupied by the buttery and the pantry, which lay on either side of the passage from the kitchen. The buttery contained the supplies of ale and wine, decanted for use in the hall, and the pantry contained the bread supplies. The buttery, kitchen passage and pantry emerged into the screens passage of the hall through three separate doors; the stone jamb of the right-hand door survives.

A further wooden staircase leads to the second floor, passing over the base of a spiral staircase, which was the original means of access upstairs. The surviving room was the inner chamber of a suite of lodgings, equipped with a fireplace. The polygonal room in the turret served as a bedchamber, and later provided the inspiration in Sir Walter Scott's novel *Kenilworth* for the 'small octangular chamber' in 'Mervyn's Tower' in which Amy Robsart, first wife of Robert Dudley, stayed during her fictional visit to Kenilworth (see page 23). The lodgings were designed for a senior household officer, probably the steward, because the various spiral stairs gave him direct access to the services and to the hall.

From the south door of the lodgings the south-west spiral staircase leads down to two strong-rooms, which were probably used for storing pewter, plate and other valuable items needed in the hall. Visitors should also ascend to the top of the tower for the best panoramic views of the castle and the site of the mere. The Pleasance lay at the far end of the mere, beyond where the group of buildings at High House Farm now stands in the middle distance. Originally the tower was one storey higher, like the Saintlowe Tower to the left.

8 GREAT HALL

John of Gaunt's great hall was the architectural masterpiece of the inner court, designed to symbolize his regal status. It is no wonder that this was the only part of the castle left unaltered by Leicester 200 years later, for it entirely suited the image he wished to project.

Exterior

The building is six bays long, with the bay window on the left balanced by the porch on the right. The windows are noteworthy for both their exceptional height and their delicacy; they are more like cathedral windows. Each is divided by horizontal transoms into three sections. The rectangular lights were originally barred and shuttered, while the tracery in the upper section had the luxury of fixed glazing. This tracery is the best surviving example of the early Perpendicular style in a domestic building. It is similar to the tracery in the contemporary chapter house of the earl of Warwick's new collegiate foundation at St Mary's Church, Warwick.

The hall itself was on the first floor, raised over stone-vaulted cellars, and its porch was originally approached up a long straight stair of 20 steps. The entrance arch, which is ostentatiously carved with rows of foliage, led into the screens passage at the low end of the hall.

Interior

The ground-floor entrance leads to the site of the cellars. Here there were two rows of pillars at 15 feet (4.6m) intervals, supporting the rib vaulting on which the hall floor once rested. The north end of the cellars was taken up by a cross-passage to a small exit, secured by a portcullis, which provided an alternative route from the inner court to the water gate on the edge of the mere. In the 1563 survey, the wine cellar and the beer cellar occupied the rest of the space under the hall, like the contemporary arrangement at Hampton Court Palace.

Above, the magnificent interior of the hall was dominated by its deep-set windows, all of which featured panelled surrounds and stone seats. Benches would have been put against the walls to create a step up to the seats, from which spectators could watch entertainments after a banquet. The bare panels of wall above the fireplaces would have been hung with tapestries, which were among the most prized possessions of 14th-century aristocrats. Gaunt's hall was exceptional in once having no fewer than six fireplaces. Besides the two surviving fireplaces, there was a group of three fireplaces on the far wall, now destroyed. This feature was at the cutting edge of architectural fashion. The hall of Gaunt's

Great hall exterior

A Bay window
B Window tracery
C Plinth mirroring that of great tower
D Entrance arch

Below: The chapter house at St Mary's Church, Warwick, is contemporary with the great hall and has similar window tracery

**Great hall interior
(east side)**

A Hall cellars
B Entrance to the hall
C Perpendicular
window tracery
D Fireplace with wall
above for tapestry
E Large wall-slots for
the roof trusses
F Site of the
bay window

eldest brother, the Black Prince, at Kennington Palace in Surrey, dating from about 1358, probably had a similar triple fireplace. The sixth fireplace at Kenilworth is in the bay window.

The duke would have dined in the hall only on the most important of occasions. Food would have

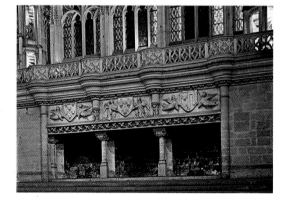

Right: A magnificent example of a triple fireplace in the hall of the ducal palace at Poitiers, France (1380s), built for John of Gaunt's contemporary, the duke of Berry

been brought in from the screens passage – a corridor across the kitchen end of the hall, created by a wooden screen. The serving of food was the most elaborate ritual which took place in the hall, permitting a lavish display of hospitality. Musical accompaniment was a significant feature, and Gaunt retained his own company of musicians. His hall probably had a minstrels' gallery over the screens passage, and one definitely existed in Leicester's time.

The rapid pace of change in 14th-century architectural fashion is shown by the fact that Gaunt's hall was the third on this site in 60 years. Thomas, earl of Lancaster, had built a 'new hall' in 1313–14, which would have been a ground-floor hall, with internal arcades to support the roof. In 1347 his nephew, Henry of Lancaster, had the hall remodelled. A London carpenter, Richard de

Felstede, was contracted to make a new roof, which suggests a major work, probably involving the removal of the arcades and the creation of a single-span roof.

A generation later (between 1373 and 1380) Gaunt had Henry's hall almost totally rebuilt so as to raise it on cellars, on the model of Edward III's new hall at Windsor. Some features from the 1347 hall might have been reused, such as the carved stone entrance doorway, but the roof was apparently replaced. No record of its design survives, but it remained the widest roof of any royal hall in medieval and Tudor England, save only for the quite exceptional roof of Westminster great hall. Like that at Westminster, Kenilworth's great hall would have been prominent in the tradition of such buildings, a visible external symbol of Gaunt's wealth and hospitality.

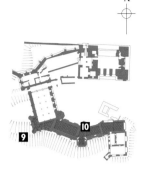

N

9 SAINTLOWE TOWER

At the south end of the hall is the Saintlowe Tower, a name used by Sir Walter Scott for a fictitious Norman founder of the castle. The ground floor was a cellar, used to supply wine to the high end of the hall, by way of the corner stairs.

The first floor forms a gallery with large windows and fitted seats looking over the chase and the mere. The stairs originally continued to a superior set of lodgings on the second floor. These might have been for the chamberlain, who was in charge of the apartments and private chambers. In the space below was a lodging for another official, perhaps the clerk of the wardrobe.

From the first-floor gallery, there is a good view of the range of state apartments on the south side of the inner court. This gallery once led to the first apartment, the great chamber. At the far end of the great chamber was a lobby, linking to the second chamber.

Below: The Saintlowe Tower seen from the outer court. The large windows are for the viewing gallery

10 STATE APARTMENTS

Return to the inner court, and proceed across it to stand near the front of the oriel, the central, projecting feature of the medieval apartment range.

The state apartments were on the first floor, and are difficult to appreciate now because since 1649–50 their fabric has been almost totally removed. They can be reconstructed from surveys of the castle taken in about 1545 and 1563, though room names and functions changed somewhat between the 14th and 16th centuries. The three main rooms were the great chamber, the second chamber (1545) or presence chamber (1563), and the privy chamber. These rooms were for the use of the lord of the castle, and those that were furthest from the hall were the most exclusive.

Exterior

The features still standing provide evidence for two main periods of work: Gaunt's and Leicester's. The central oriel, Gaunt's Tower behind it, the great

The state apartments seen from **Saintlowe Tower**

A Central oriel
B Former windows of the great chamber
C Site of wardrobe (beneath the great chamber)
D Gaunt's Tower
E Privy kitchen (beneath the second chamber)

Left: The central oriel, which formed the entrance to the state apartments. The entrance from the inner court is on the right, and the 14th-century windows on the floor above lit the first-floor lobby to the state apartments

Below: A detail of an 18th-century painting, by Paul Sandby, of Edward III's royal lodgings at Windsor, showing the 'La Rose' Tower, the model for the oriel at Kenilworth, on the left

chamber (to the right), and probably the second chamber (to the left) were all built for John of Gaunt in the 1370s. That the great chamber is on the site of an earlier chamber can be deduced from the fact that a 13th-century window survives at the north end of its basement. About 1570–71 the apartment range was renovated for Leicester. The veneer of the new masonry on the outside of the building is visible at the junction with the bay window in the great hall. The foundations of two Elizabethan bay windows survive between the hall and the central oriel, and there are also fragmentary remains of a new oriel between the second chamber and the privy chamber, which would have provided Elizabeth with a direct route to her accommodation in Leicester's Building.

Interior

The door of the central oriel leads into a room which is remarkable for its date, in that it provided a direct link from the courtyard to the heart of

GAUNT'S TOWER

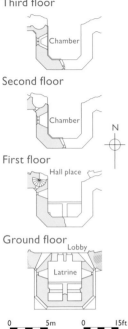

Third floor

Chamber

Second floor

Chamber

N

First floor

Hall place

Ground floor

Lobby

Latrine

0   5m   0   15ft

the private chambers, an idea derived from the 'La Rose' Tower in Edward III's lodgings at Windsor Castle. The normal arrangement would have been for the private chambers to have been approached via the great hall. A spiral staircase once led up to the first-floor 'hall place', which acted as a lobby connecting the two main chambers. From the lobby another spiral stair went up into Gaunt's Tower.

No documentation exists for the precise usage of the apartments in Gaunt's time, but it is likely that the great chamber was his audience chamber and also where the most important members of the household staff usually dined. The second chamber was probably his private dining room, and beyond this would have been the state bedchamber. Gaunt's Tower provided the duke with his most private rooms – somewhere he might relax and admire the view. By the time of Queen Elizabeth's visits in the 1570s, the second chamber had become the audience (presence) chamber, dining took place in the privy chamber (private apartment) and the state bedroom had moved into the new Leicester's Building.

The ground floor below the great chamber probably housed the wardrobe, which included precious possessions such as plate, tapestries and bed-hangings. According to William Oke, Gaunt's clerk of the wardrobe, the duke possessed 'a finer wardrobe than any other Christian king'. Beneath Gaunt's Tower the substantial latrines for the household staff are still visible. The ground floor below the second chamber appears to have been the location of a second privy kitchen which is listed in 1563, and was in an ideal location to serve food directly to the apartments above. Previously food might have been brought across the courtyard from the main privy kitchen (see page 11), via the private door in the oriel.

Down the modern wooden steps is the basement below the privy chamber. By the time of the 1563 survey there were another five chambers beyond the privy chamber, grouped around 'the king's chamber with a fair compass window of stone'. Leicester's accommodation was probably in this area during Elizabeth's visits (see page 8). The 1563 survey also appears to place 'the nursery' together with a chamber that 'sometime was the chapel' in this part of the court. Practically none of this can be identified on site now, because most of these rooms were in the lost east range. However, the stone foundations thought to belong to the chapel are still visible.

Right: A late 15th-century Flemish manuscript illustration depicting John of Gaunt (left) dining with the king of Portugal (centre), in a great chamber with serving hatch and musicians' gallery. John's daughter, Philippa, married King John I of Portugal

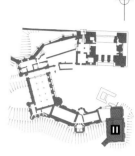

A RECONS
AT THE TI

Left: The east elevation of Leicester's Building. The windows of the principal floor, which was occupied by Elizabeth I, were destroyed after 1650

three-room s
the right-han
chamber in th
surrounds wo
stones such a
partition wall
has been lost
occupied the
chamber was
rooms enjoye

On the to
would have b
queen's danc
the east wind

▥ LEICESTER'S BUILDING

This tower block was erected between 1571 and 1572 by Elizabeth I's favourite, Robert Dudley, earl of Leicester, specifically to provide private accommodation for the queen and her close servants. She used it in 1572, and it was subsequently improved for her visit of 1575 (see page 23). To make enough space for a building which is the size of a compact country house, it was extended beyond the medieval curtain wall, the foundations of which run diagonally across the privy chamber site. At full height it was a four-storey building, but because it descends downhill and out over the former ditch, two of the floors – the ground floor and basement – were below the principal floor level.

Interior: The Northern Rooms

From the basement below the privy chamber, there is a good view into the northern rooms of Leicester's Building. They were a direct continuation of the state apartments range and were limited to three floors, unlike the rest of Leicester's Building. On the principal (top) floor was the privy chamber, denoted by the apertures for doors and fireplaces surviving in the south wall.

Right and be
Drawings ma
the Italian ar
Zuccaro, of R
earl of Leices
Elizabeth I. Th
preliminary s
complemento
the queen ar
courtier comr
Leicester spe
Kenilworth fe
The portraits
intended to h
queen's danc
in Leicester's

that 'the Coventry men' performed a play in the base court, celebrating an ancient defeat of the Danes. Elizabeth saw little of the play because she was distracted by the 'delectable dancing' within the chamber.

Below these rooms, the ground floor was also residential, but it must have been of a lesser status, as it has fireplace surrounds carved from the local sandstone. The likely occupants of this floor were Elizabeth's ladies. The bare basement rooms are clearly designed for storage, presumably for the bulkier items of her prodigious travelling wardrobe.

The door in the north-east corner leads into the basement of the east rooms. On the principal floor was the withdrawing chamber, the first room of Elizabeth's suite, and the top floor formed an ante-chamber to the dancing chamber. The physical evidence for original fittings and for the hierarchy of accommodation is especially well preserved on the internal walls of these rooms. For example, rows of small holes for wooden pegs on the south and west walls of the principal floor indicate that the queen's withdrawing chamber had a tall plaster frieze.

The north-west door from the south basement leads into the west basement. This space encompassed the service requirements for the building. A chute for sewage and waste water is built into the east wall; it drained into a culvert beneath the basement floor. Originally there were timber-framed closets on each floor. A fine wooden staircase on a square newel plan must have existed in the southern part of the space to connect the upper floors. Without it, before the south-west turret stair was added there would have been no direct link between these levels.

View of the south rooms
of Leicester's Building,
looking west

A Doors into the
    south-west
    staircase turret
B West windows
    reduced to three lights
    wide to accommodate
    addition of turret
C Elizabeth's bedroom
    and inner chamber
D Elizabeth's dancing
    chamber

LEICESTER'S BUILDING

Basement

N

Wardrobe

Wardrobe

0   5m

Ground floor

Services

Lodgings

Lodgings

Principal floor

Privy
chamber

Stairs   With-
          drawing
          chamber

Inner   Bedroom
chamber

0   15ft

Top floor

Roof

Ante-
chamber

Dancing
chamber

Turret

Left: An Elizabethan progress to Nonsuch Palace, Surrey, showing the queen's 'chariot', from a drawing by Joris Hoefnagel (1568)
Below: A medieval citole (a four-stringed instrument), engraved on the silver plate with the arms of Elizabeth I and Robert Dudley, which suggests that it may have belonged to either the queen or her favourite

Elizabeth and Leicester: the 1575 Visit

Elizabeth I enjoyed travel and made summer progresses away from London virtually every year in the first half of her reign. She had come to Kenilworth on three previous occasions before her 19-day visit between 9 and 27 July 1575, the longest stay at a courtier's house during any progress. The events can be reconstructed from a long letter by Robert Langham and from an account of the festivities by George Gascoigne. Langham was a member of Leicester's household, while Gascoigne was a poet and actor commissioned by Leicester to write and organize many of the entertainments.

At the start of her reign Elizabeth had been strongly attracted to Leicester (then Sir Robert Dudley), with whom she went riding almost daily. But the suspicious death in 1560 of Robert's first wife, Amy, *née* Robsart, at Cumnor Place, Berkshire, rather cooled the affair, and the established aristocracy were wary of a family which had already produced one over-mighty subject, namely Dudley's father, the duke of Northumberland. Elizabeth went on to toy with other suitors. So the staging of the 1575 visit was intended to impress Leicester's importance on the queen and represented his last extravagant fling to win her hand in marriage.

The most pointed reference was to have been Gascoigne's masque 'Zabeta', a play on the name 'Elizabeth'. The story hinged on a debate about whether the chaste nymph, Zabeta, should wed, and concluded with a speech urging the queen to marry.

It was cancelled, however, ostensibly because of bad weather. Not to be outdone, Gascoigne improvised a farewell to the queen, where she was intercepted by 'deep desire' (an actor dressed as a prickly holly bush, representing Leicester), who urged:

> Live here, good Queen, live here;
> you are amongst your friends.
> Their comfort comes when you approach,
> and when you part it ends.

Although Elizabeth retained her affection for Leicester, her 'sweet Robyn', she never returned to Kenilworth. In 1578 Leicester secretly married Lettice Knollys, countess of Essex, and Elizabeth was furious. He returned to favour in the 1580s, however, and as he lay dying in 1588, he wrote a letter to Elizabeth which she kept in a casket by her bed until her death, marked simply 'his last letter'.

In the 19th century Sir Walter Scott added a new twist to this love story in his romantic novel, *Kenilworth*. He had Amy still alive in 1575, and being smuggled into the castle to shame the unfaithful Leicester before Elizabeth and ruin his plans.

Elizabeth's 19-day visit to Kenilworth in 1575 was her longest stay at a courtier's house during any progress

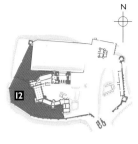

*Right: William Dugdale's
plan of the castle (1656), with
all the castle buildings listed
at the bottom*

Below: The compass window

*Bottom: View of the castle
painted by J M W Turner in
about 1830*

*Facing page: The great hall,
seen from the left-hand court,
with the Strong Tower (left)
and Saintlowe Tower (right)*

🔢 OUTER COURT

The 1563 survey divides the outer court into three areas: the 'base court', the 'court at the left hand' and the 'court of the right hand'. These divisions are still visible, with the gate to the left court adjacent to Leicester's Building and with the right court largely occupied by the garden. Their former existence emphasizes the structured layout of the castle plan, with the more public activities taking place in the base court, and the more private areas grouped in the left and right courts.

Left-hand Court

The tour of the left-hand court starts outside the basement of Leicester's Building, by the wall which originally held the gate to the left-hand court. Ahead, the dominant feature immediately to the right is the multi-faceted exterior of Gaunt's Tower, rising from a basement which houses the cesspit for its latrines. Beyond it is the base of the splendid 'compass' window, which lit the high end of the Elizabethan great chamber, supported on a restored buttress. From the far end of the court there is a good view of the west elevation of the great hall, flanked by the Strong and Saintlowe towers; the symmetry and verticality of Gaunt's buildings can be appreciated from here.

The mound in front of the great hall was a pre-existing feature, which was heightened at some time after the hall was built, perhaps as a terrace for watching entertainments on the mere.

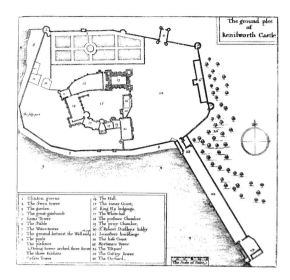

Adjoining the water gate in the outer curtain wall is the best-preserved length of wall, which retains window and fireplace apertures of various dates – testimony to the domestic buildings once contained in the left-hand court. The 1545 survey states that 'about the walls there be houses built for 200 persons to lodge in'.

Right-hand Court

Through the arch in the dividing wall between the left-hand and right-hand courts is the site of the structures marked on Sir William Dugdale's plan of 1656 as the 'plesance' buildings. Apertures for fireplaces are still visible against the north face of the wall. These buildings, which had been salvaged from the 'Pleasance in the Marsh' (see page 44), were probably not the same as those erected in the base court in 1524 (see page 45).

Further along the outer curtain wall is the so-called King's Gate, an entrance introduced at some date after 1650 for agricultural use, but reusing medieval stones. The Swan Tower, at the north-west corner of the curtain wall, was already called 'le Swannesnest' in 1439–40 and was presumably so named because of swans on the mere. Its original structure dates to about 1210–15, but little survives above basement level. Elizabethan details in the stonework suggest that the top floor was converted by Leicester into a banqueting house, to take in the view of the mere, and perhaps as an adjunct to the garden.

The path up the steps leads to the Elizabethan garden (see page 30). On the far side of the garden is Leicester's Gatehouse.

Above left: The stable seen from Leicester's Gatehouse. It was restored in the 1970s; its previous appearance is shown in the photograph below

Above right: The interior of the stable in use as 'Lord Leicester's Barn Restaurant' in the early 1930s. The diagonal braces supporting the roof trusses were removed in the 1970s restoration

Below right: The stable forms a backdrop for a practice of the Home Guard during the Second World War

🄴 STABLE

The path downhill from the gatehouse leads to the stable. A stable is documented at the castle from at least the early 14th century, but the present building was erected in 1553 for Leicester's father, John Dudley, duke of Northumberland. Described in the 1563 survey as 'a very fair and a strong new stable which my lord's grace your father made … in length 180 feet and in breadth 21 feet', it remains an outstanding survival from a period when grand stable buildings were becoming the fashion. From 1650 until the Victorian period the building continued in use as a stable and barn, as part of the farm established in the base court.

The ground floor is built of good ashlar (square-cut stone) against the earlier curtain wall of the castle. Its original features include the porch,

two doorways to the north and the windows (the larger ones were modified later). The large south entrance was rebuilt in brick in the early 19th century. The upper storey is of timber-framed construction, with decorative square panelling along the west face, which was restored in the 1970s. The ornamental timber braces are specifically in the form of ragged staves, the Beauchamp device adopted by Northumberland and Leicester. The stable building takes on further significance when we remember that both men were Masters of the Horse to Edward VI and Elizabeth I respectively.

Inside the stable, the impressive open roof of 11 bays was restored in the 17th century reusing some of the 16th-century timbers. In the 1563 survey the stable is described as having '30 rooms [stalls] for great horses besides rooms for 20 geldings'. The northern bays were still fitted with stalls and in use as a stable in the mid-Victorian period. Other details of the building's original usage are less easy to reconstruct. Initially, there was an upper floor for storage, and perhaps for accommodation for grooms. The 1563 survey notes that if the stable was 'boarded over the joists', in it 'might be laid 300 loads of hay'. During the 1930s 'Lord Leicester's Barn Restaurant' operated in the southern half of the building, a space occupied today by the café and an introductory exhibition to the castle.

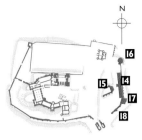

15 COLLEGIATE CHAPEL

In front of the stable lie the foundations of the collegiate chapel of St Mary, built for Thomas of Lancaster between about 1314 and 1322. It was one of the largest private chapels of its time, about 45 feet (14m) high and at least 100 feet (30m) long. Its west end is now buried under the later bank. It was possibly demolished in about 1524, when the foundations might have been reused for a timber-framed building brought from the Pleasance in the Marsh (page 44). This, in turn, was probably removed by Leicester. The only recognizable features of the foundations are the polygonal apse for the chapel's altar and fragments of a reset sedilia, the seating for priests officiating at the Mass.

16 LUNN'S TOWER

To the north of the stable is the so-called Lunn's Tower, the best preserved of King John's wall towers of about 1210–15. The ground floor was powerfully equipped with five fish-tailed arrowloops: the two that remain today have been restored, and are best seen from the exterior. The external stair turret gave access to the two upper floors and the wall-walk. The second floor was built as a residential chamber, and the first floor was subsequently converted into another chamber.

A two-storey timber building was once connected to the tower. It was probably the house built by the constable, John Ashford, which in 1400 was confirmed in the possession of his wife, together with 'the tower adjoining'. The constable was permanently resident at the castle and responsible for its security.

17 WATER TOWER

To the south of the stable is the Water Tower, so called because it overlooked the lower pool. It was probably built by Thomas of Lancaster in the early 14th century. Its exterior has pyramidal corner buttresses and cruciform arrowloops with oillets (eyelets), characteristic of the period.

The tower provided additional lodgings for Thomas's leading retainers. The ground-floor door led into a private chamber with a fireplace and latrine. An internal spiral stair gave access to a superior first-floor chamber, which has two-light windows with built-in seats. The rows of holes cut into the interior walls relate to its use as a 'pigeon house', as documented in 1748.

LUNN'S TOWER

Ground floor — First floor — Second floor

Blocked loop — Chamber — Chamber

0 ___ 5m   0 ___ 15ft

18 OUTER CURTAIN WALL

The surviving length of the outer curtain wall, which runs towards Mortimer's Tower, retains features indicating that there were once buildings adjacent to the wall. A residential chamber in the thickness of the wall is equipped with a latrine and a fireplace, probably dating from the early 14th century. The 1563 survey also records a brewhouse, water mill and bakehouse in this area of the outer bailey.

Left: The exterior of Lunn's Tower, commanding the north-east corner of the outer curtain. On the ground floor is a Victorian restoration of a fish-tailed arrowloop, and at the top left is a latrine chamber discharging into the moat

Below left: The Water Tower, added to the outer curtain in the early 14th century, has distinctive pyramidal corner buttresses and a projecting chamber at ground-floor level for a latrine (right). The large round-headed aperture between them is a modern modification

WATER TOWER

First floor

Chamber

Ground floor

Chamber

0 ___ 5m   0 ___ 15ft

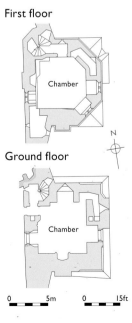

The Elizabethan Garden

During Elizabeth I's reign, elaborate formal gardens and extensive pleasure grounds became an essential accessory of the great house. They continued the medieval tradition of evoking an earthly paradise, but they were much more – a place to display their owner's pedigree, to entertain and feast, and to evoke the legends of classical antiquity. Most of all, they came to represent the cult of Elizabeth, with various flowers and other features chosen to reflect her regal virtues.

Gardens are known at other great Elizabethan houses, but as at Kenilworth they have all disappeared except for some earthworks. For more than 400 years the Kenilworth garden created for the queen by Robert Dudley, earl of Leicester, was lost, but it has now been reinstated by English Heritage – the first ever recreation of an Elizabethan garden on such a scale.

Left: The Elizabethan garden, recreated by English Heritage in 2009, looking from the terrace towards the fountain and aviary

Facing page: Planting around one of the obelisks, which stand in the centre of each quarter of the garden. According to Robert Langham the obelisks were carved from porphyry, a rare purple marble from Egypt, although they are more likely to have been painted timber, as now recreated

INTRODUCTION

The garden that greeted Elizabeth on her visit to Kenilworth in 1575 (see page 23) is the first of her reign for which we have detailed evidence, thanks to a remarkable eyewitness account by Robert Langham, an official in Leicester's household, in a letter to his friend Humphrey Martin in London. Although it was a privy garden, for the queen and her companions only, he relates how with the connivance of Adrian the gardener he sneaked in one day when 'the garden door was open and her highness out hunting'. He describes all the main features which have now been recreated – the terrace, the arbours, the marble fountain, the aviary, and the giant obelisks.

Leicester paid as much attention to improving the surrounding landscape as he did to his new buildings and garden. The garden was just part of a larger setting for the queen's entertainment, which spread over the park, the chase and the mere. The park lay to the south-west of the castle and the chase stretched to the north and west, with the mere between them. Both park and chase were heavily wooded and well stocked with red deer and other game, such as pheasants. Together with wild fowl on the mere, they probably constituted the main attraction of Kenilworth for Elizabeth, who loved hunting with hawks and hounds.

Leicester's lavish series of entertainments for the queen in 1575 made full use of this landscape. For example, as Elizabeth was returning from hunting in the chase one evening by torchlight, she was confronted by the dramatic spectacle of a 'wild man' covered in moss and ivy; in a poetic dialogue with the nymph, Echo, he revealed that the gifts Elizabeth had received were 'tokens of true love' from Leicester. The festivities also included a dramatic firework display one night across the mere, in which some fireworks 'burnt unquenchable under the water'. On another evening a play involved a figure of Triton riding a mermaid 18 feet long and the Lady of the Lake with her nymphs on moving islands.

Langham tells us that the tall, fragrant trees gracing the landscape might have pleased Diana, the goddess of hunting and chastity often associated with Elizabeth; for Langham, the pleasure grounds were evidently a setting for interplay between mythological and real figures. Leicester beautified this natural landscape with 'many shady bowers, arbours, seats and walks'; it was the queen's custom to watch the hunt from a seat in an arbour. Another important feature was the new wooden bridge across the northern arm of the mere, which provided not only a more direct link between the chase and Leicester's Gatehouse but also a viewing platform over the mere.

'a garden so appointed to feel the pleasant whisking wind above, or delectable coolness of the fountain-spring beneath; to taste of delicious strawberries, cherries, and other fruits … to smell such fragrancy of sweet odours, breathing from the plants, herbs, and flowers; to hear such natural melodious music and tunes of birds'
Robert Langham, describing the garden in 1575

One of the obelisks, modelled on the originals as described by Langham

The west arbour

All the plants now growing here would have been available in Elizabethan England, and the planting is designed to peak each year in July, the month of the queen's visit in 1575

Opposite: *Detail of the marble fountain, which takes the form of two Athlants (mythological giants who held up the sky) supporting a sphere, and is the dramatic focus of the garden*

TOUR OF THE GARDEN

■ Terrace

Today the visitor approaches the garden along the same privileged route taken by Elizabeth, through the classical loggia of the forebuilding, which leads on to the terrace. Reconstructed to its original height, the terrace affords the best view of the garden and the landscape beyond. Set at intervals along the terrace balustrade are obelisks, spheres and Leicester's badge of the bear and ragged staff.

The garden below is divided into quarters, and the alleys in between were according to Langham 'green by grass … and some with sand smooth and firm, pleasant to walk on like a sea-shore'. In the centre of each quarter stands a pierced obelisk 15 feet (4.6m) high, an ancient symbol of power and immortality.

■ Arbours

At each end of the terrace are the 'two fine arbours', which Langham noted were 'perfumed by sweet trees and flowers'. Reconstructed from an engraving by the 16th-century French architect and designer Jacques Androuet du Cerceau, they are planted with vines, honeysuckle and the sweet musk rose associated with the cult of Queen Elizabeth. Langham extolled the pleasure of walking on the terrace, breathing the scent of the plants, enjoying the views of the mere and the chase, and looking from the east arbour on to the people in the base court below.

■ Planting

In an Elizabethan formal garden, with all its man-made features, the plants were almost incidental. Langham says little about the plants at Kenilworth, so these have had to be reconstructed from other contemporary documentary and visual sources, such as tapestries made for Leicester. Langham's emphasis on the sweet scent from 'the fragrant herbs and flowers' suggests that it was a fashionable 'gillyflower' garden, popular in Elizabeth's reign. Gillyflowers are perfumed perennials, such as carnations, pinks, stocks and wallflowers.

Each quarter is subdivided into two knots, with intricate geometrical patterns of planting based on contemporary drawings by the Flemish architect and garden designer, Hans Vredeman de Vries. Four patterns are used, repeated in the east and west halves of the garden. The quarters are fenced in,

and hedged with a mixture of hawthorn, privet and the prickly eglantine rose, which would have been used to keep out dogs and other animals. The knot patterns are delineated by low hedges of English privet, bordered with such plants as pink thrift and, in summer, wild strawberry. The focal points of each knot are planted variously with small trees and shrubs – bay, holly, juniper, viburnum and rose.

Langham mentions cherries, pears and apples, which probably included French varieties, because plant cultivation in France and Italy was far in advance of England at the time. The reconstructed garden has been planted with a number of traditional English varieties of fruit trees. One local variety, planted at the corners of the four quarters, is Black Worcester, a hard, round pear that would have lasted through the winter and was cooked rather than eaten fresh.

Leicester's badge of the bear and ragged staff, from his tomb in St Mary's Church, Warwick. The abundance of his heraldic devices in the garden emphasized the noble ancestry of the Dudley family

4 Fountain

The fountain is the spectacular centrepiece of the garden. Like the original, the newly commissioned fountain is made of white Carrara marble from Tuscany in Italy. Langham described the basin as octagonal and with a central column in the form of two 'Athlants' supporting a 'boll' which discharged continual jets of water; the whole was topped by Leicester's ragged staff badge.

In 1575 several varieties of fish in the basin – carp, tench, bream and perch – complemented the marine theme of the panels around it. The panels are carved with eight scenes from the Roman poet Ovid's narrative poem the *Metamorphoses*, which weaves the lives and loves of gods and mortals and describes their transformations, often into animals and plants. Langham described five of the panels as depicting Neptune with his trident; Triton (son of Neptune) drawn by fishes; Proteus (another son of Neptune) 'herding sea-bulls'; Doris and her daughters, the Nereids (sea nymphs); and Thetis (one of those daughters) in her chariot drawn by dolphins. Three additional scenes have been created to complete the panels, based on contemporary prints. The characters and stories represented are, anticlockwise from the panel facing the terrace: Neptune; Caenis and Neptune; Thetis; Perseus and Andromeda; Triton; Proteus; Doris; and Europa.

The first English edition of the *Metamorphoses* (1567) was dedicated to Leicester, and its earthy humour was enjoyed by the Elizabethans. Langham noted with amusement the sudden spouts of water which could be contrived 'at the twist of a stopcock' to soak any unfortunate spectator 'found so hot in desire' from viewing the scenes on the panels.

One of the panels around the base of the fountain, depicting the god Triton

5 Aviary

The aviary particularly drew Langham's attention and his detailed description is the first of an aviary in England. The exterior was articulated by two tiers of classical orders, and it was almost certainly built from timber as reconstructed. He admired the top cornice painted to look as though it had been 'beautified with great diamonds, emeralds, rubies and sapphires' and enthused about the songs and colours of the 'lively burds' – English, French, Spanish, 'Canarian, and (if I am not deceived) some African'. All the birds in the reconstructed aviary are domesticated. The lizard canary is the closest tame relation to the wild canary found in this period.

Birds selected for the aviary include African guinea fowl, shown here in a tapestry made for Leicester, representing species introduced into Europe in the Elizabethan period

Above: *A portrait of Elizabeth I by Marcus Gheeraerts the Elder, about 1585. In the background is the garden at Wanstead House, owned by Leicester and almost contemporary with the garden at Kenilworth*
Below: *A design for a fountain, from a tapestry made for Leicester in about 1585*

HISTORY OF THE GARDEN AND LANDSCAPE

The park and mere are the earliest documented features of the Kenilworth landscape, both being mentioned in the confirmation charters of the priory of about 1125; the mere was enlarged to its full extent about 1210–15. The hunting and recreational facilities at Kenilworth were appreciated by the earls, dukes and kings of the house of Lancaster, and a 'Pleasance' was built for Henry V on the edge of the chase in about 1417 (see page 45). The chase was vastly extended by Thomas, earl of Lancaster, in the early 14th century and Leicester acquired additional lands for it in about 1570.

The first reference to a garden at the castle is in John of Gaunt's time in 1374, and in 1463 Edward IV commanded 'a jousting place' to be made in the middle of a garden. Both these references may be to the site of the present garden, and almost certainly the 1575 garden

was not the first in this location. So when Leicester remodelled the adjacent forebuilding of the great tower with its classical loggia in about 1569, presumably he was already planning a new garden. It is likely that features such as the marble fountain and aviary were created in 1575, given their relative novelty in England, while others, such as the earthwork of the terrace, were already in existence.

The 1575 garden drew inspiration from French and Italian Renaissance models, such as the famous Tivoli gardens at the Villa d'Este near Rome, laid out in the 1550s. The classical aviary and the obelisks are among the first recorded appearances of these continental features in an English garden, and water jokes were also popular in Italian gardens. The designer of the 1575 garden is unknown, but a possible candidate is Leicester's gardener, Adrian, who is thought to have been French and would have brought with him knowledge of continental gardening techniques. The fountain is one of a number created for royal palaces during Elizabeth's reign, but was exceptional in being carved in Italian marble: the sculptor may have been the royal craftsman Cornelius Cure.

After Leicester's time, some changes may have been made to the garden under the early Stuart kings, but little survived the Civil War except the fountain, which disappeared shortly afterwards. About 1650 the mere was drained and much woodland was cut down in the park and chase, to create the arable farmland seen today. The privy garden site was given over to a kitchen garden and orchard to serve the tenants of the gatehouse right up to the early 20th century. In 1975 a Tudor garden was planted on the site, based on Sir William Dugdale's plan of 1656 (see page 24). Subsequently it became evident that the roots of the plants were destroying what archaeology remained, so in 2004 English Heritage commissioned a programme of research to inform a more authentic recreation of the 1575 garden.

The archaeological excavations of 2005–6 revised Dugdale's plan by revealing that the centre fountain was on an axis with the forebuilding and that the 1575 garden was shorter than in his plan. The accuracy of Langham's account of the fountain was borne out by the discovery of the foundations of its 'eight square' (octagonal) basin in the centre

Left: This design of 1576 for an ornamental garden, by Hans Vredeman de Vries, provides a close parallel with the garden at Kenilworth, with its arbours and shaped flower beds
Below: An arbour being built as a shade against the sun, from The Gardener's Labyrinth, *1586*

of the garden and chips of 'hard white marble' (Carrara) on the spot. Langham's descriptions are not always clear or complete, however, and require interpretation. The Athlants of the reconstructed fountain support a ball (sphere), but Langham's 'boll' could equally have been a bowl. His architectural description of the aviary has had to be fine tuned by reference to the classical details of the contemporary porch on Leicester's Gatehouse. His claim that the obelisks were carved from porphyry is unconvincing: it is more likely that, as now reconstructed, they were made from timber painted to look like porphyry. A survey of 1609 lists 'the queen's seat of freestone' in the garden, but Langham fails to mention it and it has not been reconstructed.

Visitors can also view the site of the former pleasure grounds beyond the castle walls from the top of the Strong Tower (page 12) and follow public footpaths to the site of the Pleasance (not English Heritage) and vestiges of the chase – Chase Lane and Chase Wood.

History

The first castle at Kenilworth was constructed in the early 1120s on land granted by Henry I to one of his officials, who set about building a formidable defensive stronghold here. By the 1170s Kenilworth was judged to be of such strategic importance that it was taken into royal control. Henry II and King John both strengthened its defences, and in 1266 Kenilworth withstood the longest medieval siege on English soil.

In the late 14th century John of Gaunt – the greatest nobleman in late medieval England – turned this defensive stronghold into a sumptuous residence. Two hundred years later Robert Dudley, earl of Leicester, lavished a fortune on turning Kenilworth into a palace fit to entertain Elizabeth I.

This proved to be the high point of Kenilworth's history. After the Civil War, when Parliament ordered the castle to be slighted, Leicester's Gatehouse was retained as a private residence, but the rest of the castle fell into ruin.

THE DE CLINTONS: 1120–74

Geoffrey de Clinton established the first castle on this site at Kenilworth in the early 1120s. Geoffrey was chamberlain and treasurer to Henry I (1100–35), on whose support he depended entirely for his advancement. Henry had suspicions in 1119 about the loyalty of Roger, the new earl of Warwick (1119–53), and so he promoted Geoffrey in Warwickshire to counter Roger's influence. Geoffrey held the royal post of sheriff by 1121, and by 1124 he was established as a great magnate in the county. He was granted lands in the royal manor of Stoneleigh: on one part of this he established Kenilworth Castle and on the other, downstream from the castle, he founded Kenilworth Priory, in or before 1124.

It has been speculated that Geoffrey's castle was only a motte (mound) of earth crowned by timber buildings. Yet a strong case can be made to show that the existing stone great tower must have been constructed in the favourable circumstances directly after 1124. An undertaking on this scale could not have been achieved without royal resources, and in these years Geoffrey enjoyed the undiminished favour of King Henry. In 1130, however, his relationship with the king began to sour. At Geoffrey's death, in about 1133, his son and successor, Geoffrey II, was a minor, and by then the power of Roger, earl of Warwick, was in the ascendant in Warwickshire. Geoffrey II and his uncle, William de Clinton, came to an accommodation with the earl, which included Geoffrey's marriage to the earl's infant daughter, Agnes. His independence was weakened further from 1135, following the accession of King

Stephen (1135–54) and the beginnings of civil war in England. During his career, Geoffrey II never commanded the resources to undertake major works at Kenilworth or at the other de Clinton castle of Brandon, near Coventry.

Brandon Castle provides an important clue that the great tower at Kenilworth should be attributed to de Clinton patronage. Its distinctive plan, with projecting angle turrets and prominent intermediate buttresses, is reflected on a smaller scale in the stone great tower at Brandon, excavated in 1947. No independent dating evidence survives for Brandon, but a castle was in existence there by the time Geoffrey II married Agnes of Warwick, and it would be surprising if great towers of related design, in two castles possessed by Geoffrey I, were not both commissioned during his lifetime.

THE CROWN: 1174–1244

Kenilworth Castle was garrisoned for Henry II (1154–89) during the 'great rebellion' of his sons in 1173–4. At about the same time, Geoffrey II de Clinton died. The castle was then judged to be of such strategic importance that the king took it into royal control. At this time the castle consisted of at least the great tower with its forebuilding, and a single bailey (courtyard) approached by a causeway across a lake. During the next 70 years the castle's fortifications assumed the extent and form seen today: the outer circuit of stone walls with towers, and the dam with its outworks to control the water defences.

One result of royal ownership was that the history of the castle was to become better documented, especially through the annual returns (Pipe Rolls) of the sheriff to the exchequer: for example, the existence of a king's great chamber, a king's chapel and a queen's chamber is recorded in 1234–5 and 1241. By then, the defences were largely complete, but the accounts are less helpful about these works. Parallels with castle building elsewhere, however, suggest that they were mainly commissioned by Henry II, between about 1184 and 1189, and by his son, King John (1199–1216). The latter spent the large sum of about £1,100 on Kenilworth, mostly between 1210 and 1215, as part of a campaign to strengthen major royal castles following the papal Interdict of 1208 and his own excommunication.

Above: Henry III (1154–89), who brought the castle under royal control, depicted in a late 13th-century manuscript
Below left: The coffins reputed to be those of Geoffrey de Clinton and his son, excavated in the chapter house of Kenilworth Priory in about 1925

Facing page: A portrait of Robert Dudley (1533–88), earl of Leicester, thought to have been commissioned for Elizabeth I's visit to Kenilworth in July 1575

Kenilworth Priory

The lords of Kenilworth expected hospitality at the priory and the priors became in effect their local agents

Above: The priory ruins as they appeared in 1729, in an engraving by Samuel and Nathaniel Buck, which shows the chapter house wall (left) and the 'barn' and ruined gatehouse (right)

Above right: The west door of St Nicholas's parish church, Kenilworth, is a remarkable assemblage of Romanesque carved stones taken from the adjacent priory after the suppression

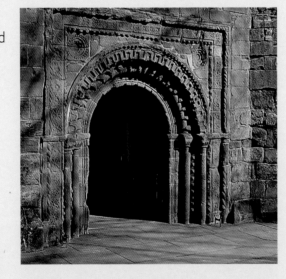

The priory of St Mary was as integral a part of the medieval landscape of Kenilworth as the castle, but its suppression in 1538 has removed its physical traces far more completely. Its few remains lie 600 yards (0.5km) from the castle, in Abbey Fields (the priory was raised to abbey status in 1447). The two structures still standing are part of the impressive gatehouse (1361–75), and the so-called 'barn' which today displays archaeological fragments from the priory. Parts of the cruciform church can also be traced, and the lake in Abbey Fields is on part of the site of the medieval fishponds.

Geoffrey de Clinton founded the priory for Augustinian canons at the same time as the castle; such associated foundations of castle and Augustinian priory were fashionable among the courtiers of Henry I. The Augustinian canons were popular with aristocratic patrons because they could render useful services beyond the cloister, a facility exploited by the lords of Kenilworth. They expected hospitality at the priory and the priors became in effect their local agents. In 1380 the prior served as the clerk of works at the castle. In June 1372, John of Gaunt ordered the priory to lay in stocks of good wine for an intended visit, and in November 1379 he ordered the relaying of the great chamber floor at the priory for dancing at Christmas. These impositions were materially worthwhile for the priory, even if spiritually questionable. It was well endowed with lands and had the second highest income of any monastery in Warwickshire at its suppression in 1538. Shortly afterwards, materials from its redundant buildings were reused in works at the castle.

The stone walls of the inner bailey date from no later than Henry II's reign, and the same is probably true of the simple stone gatehouse later incorporated into Mortimer's Tower. The presence of a gatehouse in this position must indicate the existence of an outer bailey, probably defended by a bank and ditch. King John's reign is the most likely time when the outer bailey received its present circuit of stone walls with towers. The best surviving examples are Lunn's Tower and Mortimer's Tower. The latter is an early example of a twin-towered gatehouse. As part of the same programme of extending the fortifications, the dam was heightened to enlarge the mere. Within the castle, substantial improvements were made to the great tower and a small barbican was probably added to protect the inner bailey gate.

In the end, the strength of John's castles availed him little, in the face of his unpleasant personality and an inability to manage the great barons. In 1215 he was forced to sign the Magna Carta. When John died in 1216, the French prince, Louis, invaded England in support of the rebel barons. Nevertheless,

it was the strength of another castle, Dover, that thwarted Louis' campaign, and John's young son inherited successfully as King Henry III (1216–72).

SIMON DE MONTFORT: 1244–65

In 1244 the custody of Kenilworth Castle was given to Simon de Montfort, who was granted the castle for life in 1253. Born in France about 1208, Simon was a landless younger son of Simon de Montfort the elder (about 1170–1218), the famous French crusader who had campaigned against the Albigensian heretics in southern France.

From his father, the younger Simon inherited his military ability, piety and sense of moral duty, tempered by more than a degree of self-interest. His fortunes rose rapidly after his arrival in England in 1230. He married Eleanor, the king's sister, in 1238 and was created earl of Leicester in 1239, thus regaining his family's former English estates.

When Simon was granted Kenilworth it was already an exceptional fortress, but he is reported to have strengthened it further. A chronicler refers to 'unheard of … machines' at the castle, probably the trebuchets which were to play a significant role on both sides in the siege of 1266. Simon might also have been responsible for completing the scheme of defence originally conceived by King John, by creating the Brays, the large outwork crucial to the security of the dam.

The turning point in Simon's life came in 1258, when he headed the confederacy of reforming barons against Henry III – a fateful decision which led ultimately to his defeat and death at the hands of royal forces at the battle of Evesham on 4 August 1265. After Evesham, some of his followers made a last stand at Kenilworth.

Left: The tomb effigy of King John (1199–1216) in the choir of Worcester Cathedral, supported by representations of the local saints Oswald and Wulfstan, carved in about 1230

Above: *Another early example of a twin-towered gatehouse like Mortimer's Tower at Kenilworth was King John's gatehouse at Dover Castle, shown here in a reconstruction of the French siege of Dover in 1216*

Below: *The death and mutilation of Simon de Montfort at the battle of Evesham in 1265, from an early 14th-century manuscript*

THE GREAT SIEGE OF 1266

The siege of Kenilworth Castle by royal forces in
1266 was one of the few full-scale medieval sieges
on English soil, as well as being the longest. A full
array of the latest weaponry was pitted against a
formidable modern fortress, in a type of warfare
developed by the crusaders in the Near East.

After Simon de Montfort's death at the battle
of Evesham his eldest son, Simon the younger,
promised to surrender Kenilworth to the king, but
his father's supporters inside refused. Henry III's
patience finally snapped after his messenger
returned with a severed hand. An all-out siege
began on 21 June 1266, with the garrison now
commanded by Sir Henry de Hastings (d.1268),
an outstanding leader who would maintain the
defenders' morale through great deprivation
during the next six months.

The royal forces set up stone-throwing
machines to the north, facing the great tower, and
to the south across the mere. They were thwarted,
however, by the superior range of weaponry
inside, and the king had to send to London for
larger machines. The most devastating siege
weapon of the day was the trebuchet, capable of
hurling stone balls weighing up to 300 lb (140kg)
with remarkable accuracy. In 1960 archaeologists
excavated such missiles in the outer bailey, which
had been catapulted 350 yards (320m) across the
mere and had violently destroyed a building inside
the wall. The water defences prevented the
undermining of the castle walls, so the king even
brought barges from Chester for an abortive
assault across the mere.

A parliament summoned by Henry III near the castle, perhaps on the land now called Parliament Piece, resulted in the Dictum of Kenilworth, which would permit the rebels to regain forfeited lands on payment of heavy fines. Eventually, disease and starvation brought about what the assault had failed to deliver, and the remnants of the garrison surrendered on these favourable terms on 14 December 1266.

THE HOUSE OF LANCASTER: 1266–1361

Immediately after the surrender, Henry III granted Kenilworth to his younger son, Edmund (1245–96), who was created earl of Lancaster in 1267. Thus began almost 200 years of ownership by the house of Lancaster, who were successively earls, dukes and kings, and were responsible for the distinctive development of the castle as a palace.

In 1279 it was the setting for an Arthurian 'round table', a series of tournaments and festivities based on medieval romance literature, then very fashionable among the elite of European chivalry. The celebrations were attended by 100 knights and their ladies, and the main guest was Edward I (1272–1307), Edmund of Lancaster's brother. He was there to acknowledge the farewell to arms of his close friend, Roger Mortimer. At the tournament, which may have been held in the Brays, Mortimer won the prize of a gold lion.

Edmund's son, Thomas (about 1278–1322), received a grant of his father's lands in 1298. Thomas of Lancaster entertained on a scale rivalling that of the king and maintained a household of over 500 retainers. At Kenilworth he added 800 acres (324ha) to the chase and probably commissioned the Water Tower to provide additional accommodation for his leading retainers. Furthermore, between about 1314 and 1322 a new collegiate chapel dedicated to St Mary was built by master mason Richard de Thwaites in the outer bailey of the castle. Collegiate foundations on a large scale were fashionable acts of late medieval piety, the most famous example being Edward III's foundation of St George's, Windsor (1348). Thomas planned his foundation for 13 secular priests, but he did not live long enough to establish the college and nothing more is heard of it. When he entered into open rebellion against Edward II (1307–27), the castle was taken into royal custody, and Thomas was executed in 1322 after the battle of Boroughbridge.

However, Edward II's reassertion of power was short-lived, and ironically it was Thomas's younger brother, Henry, who captured Edward II in south Wales and brought him back to Kenilworth in 1326, where he was forced to abdicate. The estates of Lancaster, including Kenilworth Castle, were formally restored to Henry in 1327. At his death in 1345 he was succeeded by his son, Henry of Grosmont (about 1310–1361), who was a comrade-in-arms of Edward III in his wars in Flanders, France and Scotland. He was a founder knight of Edward's Order of the Garter and was created duke of Lancaster in 1351. At Kenilworth he evidently remodelled the great hall. A contract of 1347 indicates that the hall was the same size as the existing great hall, providing a valuable insight into the scale of the castle's accommodation before the works of Henry's son-in-law, John of Gaunt.

Left: A mid-14th-century manuscript illustration depicting the beheading of Thomas of Lancaster in 1322
Below: The Lady Chapel of Lichfield Cathedral (built in about 1320) provides a good impression of the interior of the collegiate chapel of St Mary at Kenilworth, which also had a polygonal apse beyond the altar (see page 29)

JOHN OF GAUNT: 1361–99

John of Gaunt was the greatest nobleman in late
medieval England and the most ambitious builder
at Kenilworth since King John. The fourth son of
Edward III, Gaunt was born in 1340 at Ghent in
Flanders. He became the main force in English
government after the premature deaths of his
older brothers. In 1359 he married Blanche of
Lancaster, Duke Henry's younger daughter, and he
acquired Kenilworth Castle on her father's death
in 1361. In 1362 Gaunt was created duke of
Lancaster and took possession of his wife's vast
Lancastrian estates. Blanche died in 1368, and in
1371 he entered into a marriage of political
convenience with Constanza, daughter and heiress
of Pedro I, the recently assassinated king of Castile
and León in Spain. From January 1372, Gaunt titled
himself 'king of Castile and León'.

Thus, from the early 1370s, Gaunt literally
required accommodation fit for a king. It is no
coincidence that major works are recorded at
Kenilworth from about 1373 until 1380. Such was
his wealth that comparable works were under
way simultaneously at several of his properties,
including Hertford Castle and the Savoy Palace in
London, but Kenilworth alone survives to inform
us of the palatial quality of his architecture. In fact,
Gaunt's constant involvement in national

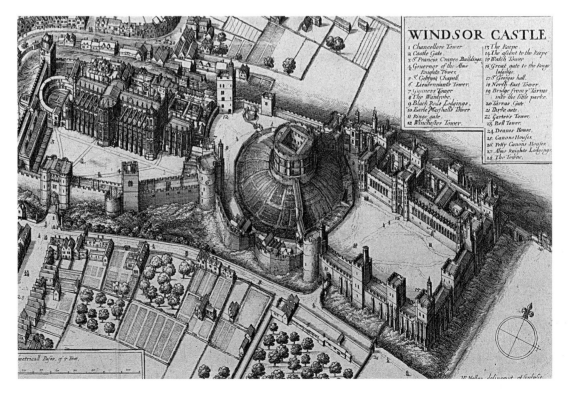

The Mere and the Pleasance

Seen across the mere, Kenilworth conjured up the image of a castle of medieval romance, encircled by water

The artificial lake known as the mere, protecting Kenilworth Castle to the south and west, was among the largest medieval, man-made water defences in Britain. A lake must have been created with Geoffrey de Clinton's castle, because a charter of about 1125 permitted the canons of Kenilworth Priory to catch fish in his 'pool' on Thursdays. About 1210 King John substantially enlarged the mere to create a body of water half a mile (800m) long and about 500 feet (150m) wide.

The mere and its associated features were not constructed just for military purposes, but were of economic benefit too. The pools supplied fish and wildfowl, and provided the power for two water mills. It was, however, the scenic and recreational qualities that came to be most appreciated. Seen across the mere, Kenilworth conjured up the image of a castle of medieval romance, encircled by water. An Arthurian 'round table' (see page 41) was held here in 1279, and during the 1575 entertainments Elizabeth I was greeted by the Lady of the Lake 'who had kept this lake since Arthur's days'.

The most extensive of the recreational facilities associated with the mere was 'the Pleasance in the Marsh' built for Henry V. This took the form of a luxurious manor house with gardens surrounded by a double moat with a harbour. The 1563 survey notes that 'in times past [the king] would go in a boat out of the castle to banquet' there, and it was

evidently designed for private entertainment. The ultimate source for the Pleasance was the garden palaces of Islamic Spain and Sicily, as emulated in northern Europe by the romantic castle and park of Count Robert II of Artois at Hesdin (Flanders, about 1300), which included a 'house in the marsh'. The Pleasance was abandoned in Henry VIII's reign and only its earthworks are visible today, standing on private farmland.

Above right: This April scene from the Très Riches Heures manuscript of the duke of Berry (about 1415) conjures up an image of the Pleasance at Kenilworth, with a walled garden and belvedere tower (right) looking back over a lake to a castle

Right: Wood engraving depicting a water pageant held to entertain Elizabeth I during her visit in 1591 to Elvetham Hall, Hampshire

government and expeditions abroad meant that he seldom visited Kenilworth, so perhaps the new work served rather to appease his wife during his flagrant adultery in the 1370s with Katherine Swynford.

The scheme for the new work was modelled on his father's new lodgings at Windsor Castle (1357–68). Both Henry Spenser, the chief mason at Kenilworth, and William Wintringham, Gaunt's master carpenter, had worked previously at Windsor. The core of Gaunt's work was the new great hall, with remodelled apartments, services and kitchens. The most innovative feature of the Windsor lodgings – the unified treatment of its main façade – finds an echo in the finely composed west elevation of the hall between the Saintlowe and Strong towers.

Extensive works at Kenilworth are also recorded between 1389 and 1393, under the local mason Robert Skillington, after Gaunt had virtually given up campaigning overseas. The projects under way were apparently of a more practical nature, involving major repairs to walls, gates and bridges, and work on the great tower 'for the safeguard of the duke's jewels there'.

THE LANCASTRIAN KINGS AND THE EARLY TUDORS: 1399–1547

The accession of Henry Bolingbroke, Gaunt's son, as Henry IV (1399–1413) brought the title and estates of the duchy of Lancaster to the Crown. Kenilworth became a favoured residence of the Lancastrian kings. It was in the great hall in 1414 that Henry V (1413–22) received the insulting gift of tennis balls from the French dauphin, provoking the campaign which led to the famous victory at Agincourt in 1415.

Henry VI (1422–71) and his queen were frequently at Kenilworth in the 1450s, as the midlands assumed a key role in the Wars of the Roses. This interest continued after the victory of Henry Tudor at Bosworth Field in 1485. As Henry VII (1485–1509) he was a regular visitor to the castle, drawn there in part by the importance of the city of Coventry and the pageants of its guilds. He and his wife Elizabeth were admitted as members of the Trinity Guild in 1499. Their son, Henry VIII (1509–47), picked out Kenilworth as one of three 'ancient castles' in the kingdom which he wished to see maintained.

Left: The Lancastrian kings depicted in the 15th-century stained glass of St Mary's Guildhall, Coventry: Henry IV (left), Henry V (centre) and Henry VI (right)

The extent of John of Gaunt's new buildings meant that the works of his successors were primarily concerned with maintenance and repairs. Such additions as were made at the castle relate mainly to the expansion of its facilities for pleasure and relaxation. For example, about 1417 Henry V commissioned 'the Pleasance in the Marsh' (see opposite) out of waste land at the far end of the mere, and in 1492–3 Henry VII had a tennis court built. Many repairs are recorded in the 15th century to the Pleasance, and eventually in Henry VIII's reign it was abandoned; at least one of its buildings – 'a praty banketynge house of tymbre' – was re-erected in the base court of the castle in about 1524. The east range of the castle's inner court, 'King Henry's Lodgings', was rebuilt in timber between 1530 and 1532, in advance of an impending royal visit.

An informative survey of the castle was made at the end of Henry's reign, about 1545. It records the castle's 'fair chambers' with 'great bay windows', 'very commodious to see the deer coursed and the fish taken'. The scene was set for the most extravagant royal entertainment at Kenilworth by Robert Dudley, earl of Leicester.

'When we have matched our rackets to these balls, We will, in France, by God's grace, play a set Shall strike his father's crown into the hazard' Henry V (shown here in a late 16th-century portrait), in Shakespeare's King Henry V, Act 1, referring to the French gift of tennis balls received at Kenilworth

'He hathe brought me
and my stocke in most
myserable callamyty
and mysery by his
exceeding ambicion'
*Lady Jane Grey of
John Dudley, duke
of Northumberland,
depicted here in
a 16th-century
Dutch engraving*

*Right: Ground-floor plan of
Leicester's proposed east
range (1568–9), superimposed
on part of the existing plan of
Kenilworth Castle*
*Below: Iron box, dated 1579,
inlaid with silver and gold and
with Robert Dudley's bear
and ragged staff badge, which
decorated many objects at
Kenilworth Castle*

THE DUDLEY FAMILY: 1547–88

John Dudley (about 1504–53) and his fourth son, Robert (1533–88), were granted Kenilworth Castle in 1553 and 1563 respectively. They had a major impact on the buildings we see today. The Dudleys rose to prominence through service to the Tudor monarchy over three generations, and on two occasions might have become kings of England themselves. John Dudley ingratiated himself with Henry VIII through military service to become the dominant force in the reign of Henry's young son, Edward VI (1547–53). John became earl of Warwick in January 1547 and duke of Northumberland in October 1551. His coup to oppose the succession of the Catholic Mary Tudor by promoting his daughter-in-law, Lady Jane Grey, ended in his execution in August 1553.

The family recovered from this setback, and with the accession of Mary's sister, Elizabeth I (1558–1603), the two surviving sons, Robert and his elder brother Ambrose (d.1590), slowly accrued offices, titles and estates. Robert was the courtier on the most intimate terms with Elizabeth during the first half of her reign, sharing her passions for riding and dancing, and she considered marrying him on several occasions (see page 23). To deserve her hand, Robert was very conscious that he needed to boost his social image. The Dudleys went to considerable lengths to trace their noble descent, especially from the Beauchamp earls of Warwick, whose territorial dominance in the midlands both Northumberland and his sons sought to recreate. Ambrose was made earl of Warwick in 1561, and Robert was created earl of Leicester and baron of Denbigh in September 1564. Both brothers, like their father, adopted the Beauchamp device of the bear and ragged staff, with which Robert emblazoned his possessions. The household inventory of Kenilworth Castle in 1588, for example, lists 'a great bedstead all painted over with crimson, and silvered with roses, four bears and ragged staves, all silvered, standing upon the corners'. The roses refer to the heraldic cinquefoil, trimmed with ermine, denoting the title of earl of Leicester.

Northumberland had formal grant of Kenilworth Castle in 1553, a few months before his death. A survey of the castle made when Robert took possession in 1563 indicates that it was Northumberland who built the existing stable

and created the tiltyard in its present form; and he would probably have made more ambitious changes to the castle, had he lived longer. He was the patron of the painter and architect John Shute, the author of the first book in English on classical architecture, and he had already remodelled the family castle at Dudley in Staffordshire.

At Northumberland's execution, Kenilworth returned to the Crown. Ten years later Elizabeth I renewed the grant to Robert Dudley, and she visited Kenilworth four times: in 1566, 1568, 1572 and finally in 1575.

Leicester soon came to appreciate the political and social importance of his midland estates, and in 1571 he founded Lord Leycester's Hospital in Warwick. As early as 1568 he was contemplating major new works at the castle, particularly replacing the Tudor east range with a vast new façade 244 feet (75m) wide (see below). The evidence comes from a plan of about 1568–9, now in the archives of Longleat House (Wiltshire), and probably drawn by the royal works architect, Henry Hawthorne. The plan would have brought an increased formality to the base court by aligning the north–south axis of the new east front with that of the stable, and by providing a grand

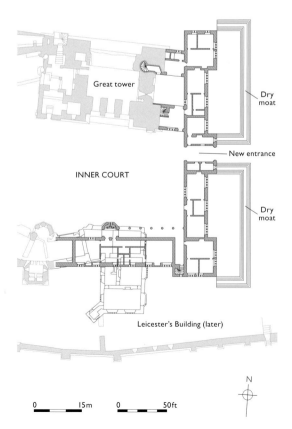

Great tower

Dry moat

New entrance

INNER COURT

Dry moat

Leicester's Building (later)

0   15m   0   50ft

N

Left: Lord Leycester's Hospital, Warwick, founded by him in 1571 as an act of local beneficence

Below: Leicester's Gatehouse, seen from the base court

entrance to the inner court. This ambitious project was never implemented, but it was the prelude to Leicester's main campaign of works between 1570 and 1572, apparently subsidized by substantial land grants from the queen.

Letters to Leicester in the summer of 1571 from his architect, William Spicer, indicate extensive works in progress on 'the new tower' (Leicester's Building), 'Caesar's tower' (the great tower) and the state apartments. Everything was being made ready for a royal visit, which materialized in 1572. The famous privy garden is not recorded until the visit of 1575, but the existence of a garden by 1572 seems probable. Elizabeth never came to Kenilworth again after 1575, but Leicester continued to visit regularly and stipulated in his will that the castle's contents were 'not to be altered or removed', as if to immortalize the events of July 1575.

Leicester's new works strove on the one hand to promote the medieval associations of the castle. The Gothic great hall of John of Gaunt was left untouched, and Leicester's new gatehouse was modelled on the Beauchamp gatehouse at Warwick Castle. On the other hand, his work also incorporated the style and luxury of the northern Renaissance, exemplified in large glazed windows, plaster friezes and ceilings, classical fireplaces and a great garden. The castle also housed a collection of

about 50 paintings, some of which he had commissioned especially for the queen's 1575 visit. The image of the castle as Renaissance country house appears in French châteaux almost certainly known to Leicester, like Gaillon (1502–10) and Ecouen (1538–55). The idea is found elsewhere in the period, for example at Ludlow and Raglan castles, but the Kenilworth remodelling was the most extensive and remains the best preserved.

The significance of the works at Kenilworth for Elizabethan architecture cannot be overstated.

Right: The effigies of Robert
Dudley and his third wife,
Lettice Knollys, on their tomb
in the Beauchamp Chapel at
St Mary's Church, Warwick
Below: Hardwick Hall,
Derbyshire (1590–97), built
by Bess of Hardwick, probably
derives its great height and
walls of glass from Leicester's
Building at Kenilworth

Facing page: A reconstruction
of the castle, viewed from
the east, as it might have
appeared in 1575, after the
earl of Leicester's works.
Since 1420 (see page 43),
Leicester's Building, the east
range and the garden have
been added, as well as
Leicester's Gatehouse (right)
and the stable against the
outer wall (foreground)

Juxtaposing Leicester's Building with the medieval
great tower meant that it had to be of
extraordinary height, creating the precedent for
the 'midland high house', of which Hardwick Hall
(1590–97) is the ultimate statement. The brittle,
thin walls and grids of windows are the prototypes
for the High Elizabethan style of the 1580s and
1590s. The scale of the accommodation also marks
out Kenilworth as the first really great house of
Elizabeth's summer progresses.

DESTRUCTION – FROM PALACE TO FARMHOUSE: 1588–1800

When Leicester died in 1588 without legitimate
male issue, almost two decades of legal and family
wranglings ensued before the castle reverted to
the Crown early in the reign of James I (1603–25).
In 1612 it was conveyed to Prince Charles, the
future Charles I (1625–49). At his marriage in 1626,
the castle was part of the marriage portion of his
new queen, Henrietta Maria, and was held in
stewardship for her by Robert Carey (1560–1639),
earl of Monmouth. The castle was well maintained
under the first two Stuart kings, and several royal
visits took place, the best known being that of
1624 when Ben Jonson's *The Masque of Owls* was
performed. Visitors noted in 1634 that the state
apartments were 'all adorned with fair and rich
chimneypieces of alabaster, black marble, and of
joiner's work in curious carved wood'.

In October 1642, soon after the beginning of
the Civil War, Charles I withdrew the Royalist
garrison from Kenilworth after the indecisive battle
of Edgehill in October 1642. The castle was then

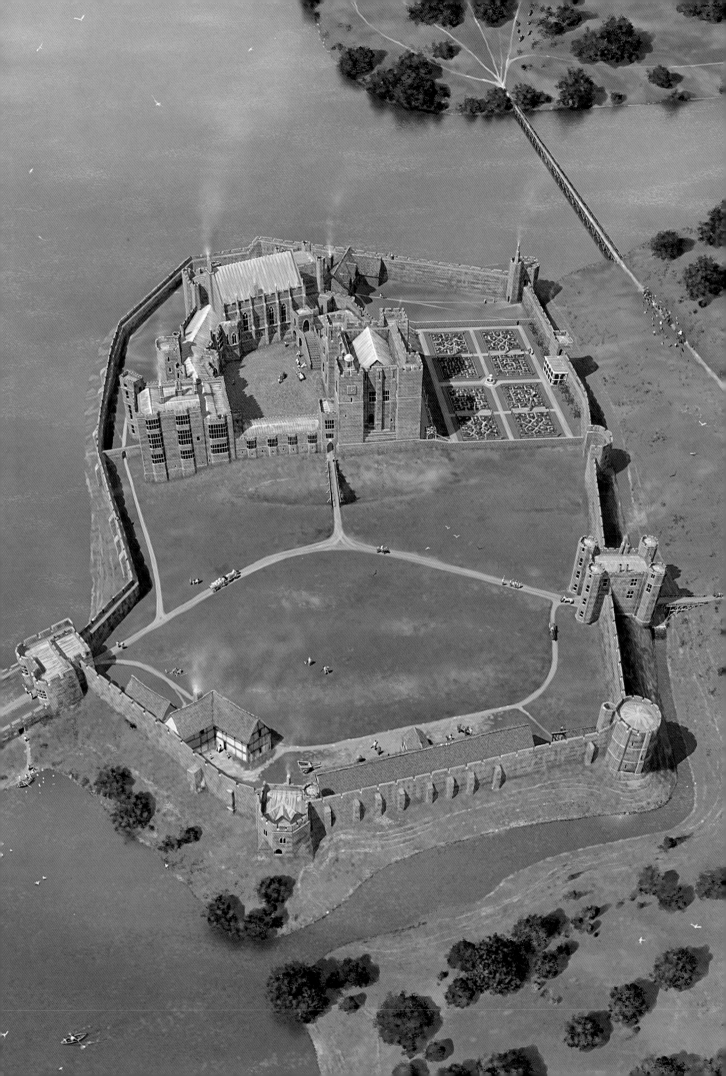

Right: Three views of the castle published in Sir William Dugdale's Antiquities of Warwickshire *(1656), engraved by Wenceslaus Hollar and based on Dugdale's own sketches. They capture the exterior of the castle in its heyday, with battlemented skylines. The top view focuses on John of Gaunt's buildings and the apartment ranges; in the middle and lower views, Leicester's Building is to the left and the great tower to the right*

Below: A view of Leicester's Gatehouse from the south-west, by Moses Griffiths, about 1779. Lunn's Tower (right) is shown still with its back wall, which collapsed about 1800

Facing page: The Death of Amy Robsart in 1560, by William Frederick Yeames, 1877. Yeames was fascinated by the events surrounding the death of Amy, Robert Dudley's first wife, and was probably familiar with Sir Walter Scott's version of the story as recounted in his novel Kenilworth *(1821)*

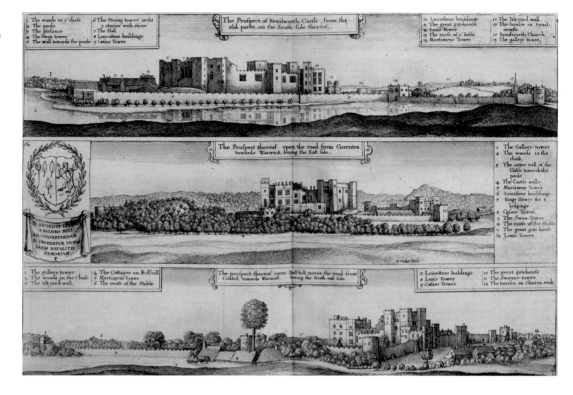

occupied by the Parliamentarians and remained largely unscathed. Following the uprisings of 1648, however, prompted by the imprisonment of Charles I, Parliament hardened its attitude to the destruction of all former Royalist strongholds. The ensuing abandonment of castles as major residences was one of the most decisive changes in the history of the English landscape. During 1649 several parliamentary orders were issued for the slighting of Kenilworth, but Henry Carey (d.1661), second earl of Monmouth, successfully petitioned 'that it be slighted with as little spoil to the dwelling house [the apartment ranges] as might be'.

In September 1649 the local antiquary, Sir William Dugdale (1605–86), made sketches of the castle, aware that it was about to be slighted. These were engraved and published in 1656 in his *Antiquities of Warwickshire*, together with the first known plan of the castle (see page 24) and a long description of its history. Dugdale's work formed the basis of all subsequent histories of Kenilworth until the later 19th century, including the nomenclature used for many of its buildings, such as Lunn's Tower, Mortimer's Tower and Leicester's Building. The slighting eventually took place in 1649–50, when the north side of the great tower was demolished and various sections of the outer curtain wall were destroyed.

Colonel Joseph Hawkesworth, the commander who had overseen the slighting for Parliament, acquired the estate in lieu of back payments for the local militia. He retained the castle for himself and converted Leicester's Gatehouse into a residence, which in due course became the house for a farm established in the bottom end of the base court. His fellow officers divided the estate into farms for themselves. The residential buildings of the inner bailey were pillaged for building materials, and the castle rapidly became a roofless ruin, with its fittings and fixtures reused in houses all round the area. At this time or shortly after, the mere was drained and

the Inchford brook returned to its natural course through a culvert in the dam.

In 1660 Hawkesworth was evicted at the Restoration of Charles II (1660–85), when the castle was restored to Charles's mother, Henrietta Maria, and for a short time to the stewardship of the earls of Monmouth. In 1665 it was granted to Laurence Hyde (1642–1711), a brother-in-law of James, duke of York (the future James II), and later earl of Rochester. In the 18th century the castle descended through his Hyde successors, and then to Thomas Villiers, who became first earl of Clarendon of the second creation in 1776. It remained with the earls of Clarendon until 1937. Their tenants continued to live in Leicester's Gatehouse during this period, using the buildings of the base court as a farmyard.

FROM ROMANTIC RUIN TO HISTORIC MONUMENT: 1800 TO THE PRESENT DAY

By the later 18th century tourists had begun to take an interest in the picturesque ruins of Kenilworth. The first guidebook, *A Concise Guide and Description of Kenilworth Castle*, was published locally in 1777, and 25 editions of it had appeared by the 1840s. However, it was the publication in 1821 of Sir Walter Scott's romantic novel, *Kenilworth*, which established the castle as a major

Kenilworth in the 1930s

From Tea at the Castle: Kenilworth in the 1930s *by Philip Hames (Odibourne Press)*

'When I was a boy we lived in Leicestershire in a large house with a big collection of antiques. In the late 1920s my family read that the gatehouse of Kenilworth Castle was to let. They decided to rent it and open it up to the public; the antiques we had would give the impression of a small stately home. We took about 25 visitors around at a time and charged one shilling each.

'At times I had the job of taking the tour. The first room entered was the dining hall, with a large table, suits of armour, and the names of the guards engraved on the left-hand side: 'Henry Butler 1649' and 'Edward Ayworth 1620'. The staircase, removed from elsewhere in the castle, led into the oak room, which was entirely panelled in oak with a large oak four-poster bed.

'At the top of the stairs was my room. When I first moved in I woke with a bad headache every morning and then found that the floor was on such a slope I had to put eight-inch blocks at the head of the bed.

'Outside the gatehouse was the barn built by Lord Leicester for stables with its fine Spanish chestnut beams. We had the idea of making it into a restaurant. It was a great success. Conducted motor-coach tours were just starting then, and they nearly all visited us. Some of the big Midland car manufacturers used to send their new cars to be photographed in the grounds.

'In front of the barn were the remains of an old wall and together with the agent to the earl of Clarendon and the curator of the castle, we started to excavate this and found what we believed to be the remains of an old chapel, which was eventually identified as the 14th-century chapel of St Mary. As we could only do this in our spare time, we never finished it, but it caused a great deal of interest and was mentioned in the papers.'

'When I was a boy ... my family decided to rent the gatehouse and open it up to the public'

Above: 'Serving wenches' in Elizabethan dress at 'Lord Leicester's Barn Restaurant' in the early 1930s
Below: The oak room, as furnished in the 1930s

Above: Repairs in progress on the great hall in the second half of the 19th century. The ground level in the foreground is considerably higher than it is today

Below right: Kenilworth Castle from the south-west, in late afternoon sunshine, which brings out the warm tones of the sandstone. For the same view painted by Turner in about 1830, see page 24

tourist attraction. Scott took liberties with history to tell a good story, but he also conveyed a convincing evocation of the castle – the 'huge pile of magnificent castellated buildings, apparently of different ages' – which he knew from first-hand acquaintance. Many thousands of visitors were drawn to see the ruins, including Charles Dickens (1838), Queen Victoria (1858) and Henry James (1870s). Lord Clarendon kept 'an aged protector' on site to deal with visitors and sell souvenirs.

At the start of the 19th century the ruins were allowed to decay, and in August 1817, 30 tons of stone crashed down from the north-west turret of the great tower. When Scott revisited the castle in 1828, he found it 'better preserved and protected', perhaps as a consequence of the interest shown after the publication of his novel. Later in the century the growing appreciation of ruins as ancient monuments, combined with the destructive aspects of mass tourism, led to efforts to arrest the decay of the castle's buildings and to investigate their history more scientifically. Foremost among the proponents of such an approach was the local antiquarian, the Revd E H Knowles, whose book, *The Castle of Kenilworth*

(1872), was the first modern, analytical account of the castle. His work benefited from clearances of rubble and restoration works undertaken in the 1860s. Whereas for many visitors 'the beauty of the ruins was heightened by the ivy which grows so luxuriantly' (Sarah Sargant, 1828), for Knowles the ivy was 'the crowbar of the giant' and 'must go'.

Substantial restorations continued in the late Victorian period and between 1926 and 1936 Lord Clarendon spent a further £10,000, but found he could not keep up with the maintenance required. So in 1937 the castle was purchased for the nation by the local motor industry magnate, Sir John Siddeley (1866–1953), who was created first Lord Kenilworth in the same year. He retained the gatehouse to live in, but placed the castle in the guardianship of the Commissioners of His Majesty's Works in 1938, giving a sum of £5,000 towards the cost of necessary repairs. In 1958 his son, the second Lord Kenilworth, gave the castle to the town of Kenilworth, and the town council remains the legal owner. In 1984 English Heritage – the distant successor of His Majesty's Office of Works – became responsible for the care of the castle, and manages and maintains it today.